Taking Refuge

Shakyamuni Buddha

Taking Refuge

A Teaching on Entering the Buddhist Path

by

Khenpo Karthar Rinpoche

KTD Publications
Woodstock, New York USA

KTD Publications
335 Meads Mountain Road
Woodstock, New York 12498

Taking Refuge is based on two teachings by Khenpo Karthar Rinpoche: "The Meaning of Refuge," given at Chicago KTC in January 1981 and "A Teaching on Refuge," given at KTD Monastery in April 1990

First Edition 2002 by Rinchen Inc., Kingston New York
Second Edition 2013 by KTD Publications, Woodstock New York

ISBN 978-1-934608-42-5
e-ISBN 978-1-934608-43-2
Printed in the USA on acid-free paper

Contents

This book is dedicated to His Holiness
the Seventeenth Gyalwang Karmapa,
Ogyen Trinley Dorje.

The Meaning of Refuge

This book is intended to give a basic understanding of taking refuge to those who are new to the Buddhist path, and to bring greater understanding to those already acquainted with it. For those who have not taken the refuge vow or have not had any involvement in the Buddhist path, there is bound to be some question as to what "refuge" is, or what "taking refuge" means and what the benefit is of taking such a vow and what it involves. Since people have different levels of understanding, this will be a very general explanation.

Given our situation as Tibetans, our talk about taking refuge could seem rather ironic. Some people may think, "What are these people talking about? They are the ones who are actually refugees! Why do we need to take refuge?" However, we are not talking about the literal sense of refuge, the idea of a general or worldly protection from something. Instead, the Buddhist concept of refuge is concerned with certain deeper realities that confront us in an ongoing way.

We all try our best to avoid these issues and pretend that we are not aware of them, but no matter what we do in the mundane world—however successful and popular we may be—certain problems and confusions will continue to confront us. Nor will these confusions be remedied by our ordinary intelligence, our ordinary ability to know and make interpretations of the world. It is possible to live our lives quite actively, to continually experience a whirlwind of activity, but in the end we must face the fact that all this activity has failed to bring any lasting meaning or purpose. At that point, all we are left with is a tremendous sense of regret and loss. As death nears, we may begin to feel alone and helpless, but hoping for protection and guidance at that time will probably not be of much help. It is important that we make preparations while there is time and while conditions are favorable.

With that in mind, we can see the need for a beginning point, an entry way to a sane and workable spiritual journey of awakening. When we take refuge, we make a genuine link with such a path, one leading directly toward liberation from our confusion and suffering both now and in the future. This journey carries with it the genuine possibility of cutting through and transforming the limitations, negative patterns, and ignorance that keep us in a state of bondage and pain.
The feeling of a need for protection is really quite universal among human beings. If you consider what has happened historically and in different cultures worldwide, you can get a feeling for the many approaches that have been tried.

Unfortunately, there is a very widespread lack of understanding as to what kind of refuge would actually serve us best. At some times and in some cultures, for example, people might see a particular mountain that seems very stable, a lake that is comforting, or a certain tree that seems to be different or unique. Because these things appear to be indestructible and beautiful, they may seem to offer that security people seek. Based on that, people may believe these sorts of things in the natural world could be suitable sources of refuge. Of course, they cannot provide any real protection.

There are others who turn to the evil beings or spirits that inhabit the world around them, assuming that these beings possess power. By seeking the protection of these forces and relating to them, people hope these spirits will become friendly and assist them. They view power as a source of protective and beneficial shelter. Yet, with evil forces there is no certainty—except that there will be evil consequences. Another misguided approach involves situations where people feel some connection or attachment, such as with friends or relatives who have died. For instance, by calling forth a dead relative or ancestor, they may hope that the relationship they had with them will cause some sort of protection or aid. It is easy to become fascinated by these things and view them as potential sources of power, benefit, or security. Again, this is of very little value.

The point is that everyone senses the need for some kind of refuge, either because of attachments or due to having a feeling of helplessness and a need for some some kind of power. As human beings, we are so dependent on our surroundings that we feel the need of some form of protection and security, yet we do not exactly know how to get this for ourselves. Therefore we try to engage in these different solutions, but to no avail.

It is unfortunate that people seek protection and refuge in these ways. Not only are these objects of refuge inappropriate—they are potentially harmful. In the worst case, in order to propitiate certain forces or entities, people may mistakenly believe it is necessary and desirable to make sacrifices. They offer the flesh and blood of beings for some imagined purpose. Sadly, these confused and harmful notions are widely held in many parts of the world.

We fail to realize that the negative experiences we go through, no matter how confusing or painful, result from our own habitual negative patterns. In addition, if we choose to indulge in further harm to others and to ourselves, we will intensify existing harmful patterns and tendencies, and increase the serious consequences.

These are not the only kinds of confusion people fall into concerning spirituality—they are just a few examples. The reason for mentioning these examples is simply this: It is extremely important to be able to discern the proper path, the proper sources of refuge, and the proper examples of spiritual sanity.

The Buddhist Approach to Refuge

As we have seen, in our search for security there are many possible mistakes we could make and sidetracks where we could become stuck. In addition, even if we are able to relate to the proper examples and the proper path, there are many challenges and possible obstacles we may encounter. With this in mind, we will now discuss the Buddhist understanding of refuge. This will be presented from the perspective of what is known as the mahayana tradition of Buddhism, the tradition of the "greater vehicle."

Our first point in this presentation is concerned with the misfortune of not having had the opportunity or desire to take refuge. In this case, we have been deprived of the benefit of the inspiration of authentic and perfect examples. In mundane existence, beings are constantly being born, only to die over and over, in fortunate and unfortunate circumstances. They are subject to rebirth because of the habitual patterns they have built up. In certain lifetimes, we may experience less confusion and we can therefore involve ourselves in some degree of wholesome activities and attitudes, which then produce beneficial situations. Other times we experience extreme confusion and negativity. By indulging these patterns more and more, we strengthen our existing habitual patterns. As a result, we go through a great deal of pain and frustration.

In general, we are continuously entrapped and bound up by this chain of confused existence, which in Buddhist terminology is called *samsara*. In samsara, we experience the fluctuations of favorable and unfavorable conditions, lifetime after lifetime. The variations in the conditions we go through mainly depend on the intensity of our ongoing confusion. This is precisely because we have not been able to relate to the proper examples or to integrate the skillful means of a proper path toward sanity and awakening. Even when we have done something wholesome and have generated some benefit for ourselves, the resulting favorable circumstances do not last and are of no permanent benefit.

This is traditionally illustrated by the image of pouring liquid into a pot without a bottom. However fresh and good it is, and no matter how much is put in, there will only be the momentary satisfaction of pouring it in, because such a vessel will not retain its contents. In the same way, no permanent benefit will come from the good we do if we lack the proper foundation.

Another image is that of sowing seeds. In order to have a fruitful crop, first there must be rich, fertile soil. Then whatever is sown will not be wasted. In our own situation, not being able to relate to the proper objects of refuge is like pouring ingredients into a bottomless pot or sowing seeds in infertile ground. As we wander in confusion, our habitual patterns become heavier and heavier and suffering becomes more intense. That is the misfortune of not having taken refuge or of not having related to proper examples of sanity and awakening.

The second point concerning the Buddhist view of refuge will be about the benefit of committing ourselves to the proper path and following the examples of the awakened objects of refuge. The buddhas and bodhisattvas, who are the embodiments of awakened compassion, started out as ordinary beings exactly like ourselves. They were not higher or better than we are, nor did they possess superior inherent qualities that we lack. Instead, by taking advantage of the opportunity to relate to the proper examples, and by sincerely committing themselves to the path that offers tremendous inspiration and encouragement, over time they became liberated. As a result of their accomplishment, they are able to benefit countless beings in skillful ways.

In the same way, we have the opportunity to free ourselves from the chain of cyclic existence (another term for samsara) by relating to the proper path and the proper examples, just as the buddhas and bodhisattvas once did. The methods they used are as fresh and as relevant as they were in the past. Once we relate to these proper sources of refuge, whatever spiritual practices we perform will be meaningful. We become fertile ground, because there is the possibility and indeed the certainty of bringing about the flourishing of positive activity. We have the capability of reaching our full potential. We are like a pot with a sound bottom, because whatever is poured in is retained, even if it is only a drop at a time.

There may be differences in our individual capacities for

understanding, but by laying the proper foundations, we are bound to experience the fruit of the practices we undertake. Once there is a solid foundation, all the benefits are lasting.

In addition, by committing ourselves to the Buddhist path we have the opportunity to fully utilize many skillful spiritual methods—first by understanding them and then by properly applying them. There are also different levels of the teachings, transmissions, and empowerments that we could receive, but unless we have been able to relate to the awakened objects of refuge, we do not have the basis for such relationships. The same is true if we aspire to practice the bodhisattva ideals: the practice of loving kindness and compassion, the cultivation of bodhicitta (the "mind of enlightenment") and the vow to work for the liberation of all beings. All this is not possible without the appropriate foundations. We may have good intentions, but not all good intentions are realistic or practical.

As we make progress in the mahayana, or bodhisattva path, there exists the possibility of being able to utilize the more advanced practices of Buddhism, the tantric or vajrayana practices. Again, however, even if we wish to learn about the application of such practices, we must first have the proper grounding to be able to fully appreciate and integrate them. Otherwise, it would be quite useless—like trying to grab hold of empty space.

In short, these are the benefits of taking refuge, of relating to the awakened examples of sanity, and of seeking awakening for both ourselves and others. I hope this communicates some of the importance of making a connection with the Dharma in the proper way.

The Three Jewels

So far we have discussed some of the possible sidetracks and misconceptions prevalent in the search for spiritual security, and the shortcomings of not taking refuge in authentic sources of refuge, as well as the benefits of doing so. Now we will take a focused look at the sources of refuge that are genuinely worthy of our commitment. These are called the awakened objects of refuge. The awakened objects of refuge are the Buddha, the Dharma, and the Sangha. The Buddha is the Awakened One. The Dharma is the teachings of the Awakened One. The Sangha is the assemblage of spiritual friends or teachers who have preserved the unbroken transmission of the Dharma. These objects are also known as the Three Jewels.

The Buddha represents complete liberation and complete awakening. As was said, the Buddha was originally an ordinary being like any one of us. His enlightenment was not something that just spontaneously occurred. He was only able to attain enlightenment by relating to the correct examples of awakening and strenuously practicing the Dharma. Therefore, he is an example for all of us that it can be done. This is why we relate to the Buddha as the ultimate object of refuge and inspiration. Going for refuge to the Buddha means relating to the state of complete awakening and being inspired by our own potential to realize such a complete awakening.

The Dharma is the path toward the experience of such liberation, as was taught by the Buddha. Just as the awakened ones made use of the path and attained enlightenment, we too can make use of the Dharma as the path toward the experience of liberation. The effectiveness of this tradition of teaching and practice in helping beings attain realization throughout history is a potent demonstration of its profound validity and effectiveness.

The third object of refuge is the Sangha, the assemblage of compassionate teachers, whom we relate to as guides on the path toward the experience of complete awakening. It was not our good fortune to be able to learn directly from the Buddha in his time. Even if we were around at that time, we were unable to take advantage of his example and his teachings. This is why the great teachers of Buddhism have preserved and maintained the unbroken lineage of the Dharma through scriptural texts, practice, and the tradition of transmission. Since the Buddha is not physically present, and we cannot expect to understand the teachings or receive transmissions of them on our own, we are kindly given the Dharma by the realized teachers who have passed the tradition down to us. Therefore, we relate to them as spiritual friends on the path toward liberation.

We could make an analogy between physical illness and the

confused condition of samsaric existence on the one hand, and between good health and the experience of enlightened mind on the other. When we are sick, we long for the experience of good health because we see the possibility of it and are inspired to get better. In that analogy, the Buddha, a fully awakened being, can be regarded as an example of complete health, and the Dharma as medicine. We realize we have some kind of sickness and we need treatment, but we are not sure what is wrong with us or how to go about treating it. Therefore, we have need of a physician who can prescribe the right medicines and stages of treatment to follow. This is how we relate to the Sangha, or spiritual friends. Once we have been cured of our illness and are experiencing good health, we no longer need treatment or a physician. In this way, we can say that the Buddha is the ultimate object of refuge, and the Dharma and Sangha are the temporary objects of the refuge.

In terms of the time span of the refuge commitment, there is some difference in motivation between the mahayana approach that we are discussing here and the approach known as hinayana, which focuses on individual liberation. We will say a bit more about this later. Although both relate to the same objects of refuge, within the hinayana motivation a person takes refuge in the awakened objects for this lifetime only. In the mahayana tradition, we remain committed to the objects of refuge from the time we take refuge until complete enlightenment has been achieved. The problem with the hinayana outlook is that it is like taking a very strong bow and arrow, aiming it at the ground right in front of you, and shooting it. It will not go very far, no matter how strong and straight it is. If you do not achieve liberation in this lifetime, what use is this commitment? With the mahayana outlook, however, the point is that when we die, the stream of mind continues on into whatever birth or stages of transformation that follow. Since the transmission is given to our mind, no matter how many lifetimes it takes to experience perfect liberation, we retain the benefit of the commitment. From rebirth to rebirth, we can thus build on prior accomplishments and go further and further on the path.

The enduring commitment of the mahayana tradition is like a seed of a flower. When the seed is planted, it does not immediately sprout, but remains hidden beneath the ground for some time, until finally a plant emerges. It takes time, but the seed is not lost–it eventually turns into a beautiful flower. Our situation is very similar. Reaching buddhahood takes time, but it is not wasted time. Therefore we take on the bodhisattva outlook in relation to time, vowing to relate to these awakened objects of refuge, these inspirational examples, until we reach enlightenment.

Looking at the motivations for refuge in terms of the scope of our aspiration, there are also basic differences between the hinayana and mahayana outlooks. According to the hinayana tradition, a practitioner relates to the awakened objects of refuge strictly for his or her own liberation, so it is a very limited scope.

In the mahayana tradition on the other hand, the motivation is much vaster because we relate to these profound examples for the benefit and liberation of all sentient beings without exception. This demands a very spacious, all-encompassing attitude. In order to be a completely responsible being, a being free from ego clinging, it is necessary for us to be responsible for others as well. Throughout time, we have been caught up in confusion and negativity because of continual attachment to self-gratification and ego clinging, which still left us extremely dissatisfied. Therefore, the best approach is to exchange our selfish attitude for the spacious, enlightened attitude of the mahayana tradition and make our commitment to taking refuge with this motivation.

The Importance of an Authentic Lineage

If we choose to receive the refuge transmission, it must come from an unbroken lineage. This means that the meaning of the teachings and of the practice has to have been immaculately preserved from the Buddha down to this day. We should only receive the transmission from such a teacher or lineage, not merely from somebody who is clever and intelligent with spiritual language. There is currently a great deal of spiritual materialism in our world, and people who know nothing about spiritual endeavors have made up many dubious teachings. Unfortunately, those who become involved with these teachings have no idea what they are getting themselves into.

As we have seen, we all have a natural thirst for spiritual wisdom. Unfortunately, people will often follow anyone making claims to spiritual knowledge. There are teachers who will make all sorts of outrageous assertions. For example, they may just rub your forehead against their own, generating some warmth, and then say, "There you go, I have now given you the transmission, because you felt it." There are others who will say, "Okay, you sit there, and I'll sit here, and you meditate, and I'll meditate, and everything will be transmitted." This sort of spiritual consumerism reflects a great misuse of the teachings.

This is why it is important that the transmission come from an unbroken lineage and from a teacher who has been authorized by such a lineage. In Buddhism there are several authentic lineages, each with its lineage holders. The lineage holder embodies the accumulated spiritual energy and realization of the lineage. Refuge needs to be given by someone—no matter how realized he or she may be—who has the formal authorization to do so from such an authentic lineage. Without this link, the actual transmission is not complete.

When we receive refuge, there is a transmission being given directly to the mind. If we merely pick up an idea and claim to have been given a mental transmission, then no benefit would result from it. For instance, if you turn on a light switch, the lamp lights because there is an unbroken wire running from it to the source of electric power. An unbroken lineage is like this. If the wire is broken, however, the lamp will not light, even if you turn on the switch. Such is the case when the lineage is broken. These are important considerations we must take into account when contemplating making a lasting commitment such as refuge.

Developing the Correct Motivation

We have seen that the purpose of taking refuge is to experience enlightenment. If we understand that enlightenment means being free of all confusion, negative psychological patterns, and lack of wisdom, we would see that there is not a single being who would not want that.

Since the experience of enlightenment is our goal, the first source of refuge is the Buddha, who is the example and embodiment of enlightenment. Taking refuge in the Buddha means that our purpose is to achieve the supreme completion of the spiritual path, just as he did. We should remember that the Buddha did not achieve enlightenment overnight—he had to follow the path of Dharma. He was originally an ordinary being, yet by following the path with diligence and enthusiasm and a sense of tremendous joy, he attained what is called *sangye* in Tibetan, which means buddhahood or perfect enlightenment.

Although we would all like to be free from all confusion and suffering and to experience enlightenment, without the Sangha, which means community, such a method as the path of Dharma might not be available in our time. It is because of the devotion of the Sangha that the path taught by Buddha has been passed down from teacher to student, and is still available in our time. Although we want to achieve the perfection of enlightenment, we will have no idea how to begin if we do not first depend on the Sangha.

Sangha members consist of those who are trained in the Dharma and have practiced and perfected some realization of the Dharma. Having that realization, they are in a position to guide the new student on the path with their knowledge of Dharma. Since the realized Sangha assists in our path toward the perfection of our goal, this is our third source of refuge. As beginners, we need to depend on the Sangha.

Understanding these three objects of refuge—Buddha, Dharma and Sangha—we also need to know that there are three ways of taking refuge, which are based on our intentions. The first way is taking refuge with a mundane or worldly aspiration. It is very common all over the world for people to take refuge with the intention of experiencing happiness, success, fame in this lifetime, or a better birth in the next lifetime. Because of lack of information or knowledge of the Dharma, these people do not know how to actually orient themselves toward enlightenment. Not knowing this, they set the goal of temporary happiness in this life and a better life in their next birth. The objects of refuge are the same—the Buddha, the Dharma, and the Sangha—and it is possible that these sorts of temporary goals for this and the next life could be fulfilled. However, these people will not be separated from the cause of suffering, since they have not aspired to go beyond samsara. They have aimed for success, good things in this life, and a better birth, but they are still within samsara, which always carries with it the potential for the experience of great suffering.

When there is the preoccupation with personal well being in this life and a better birth in the next life, these benefits may be obtained, but enlightenment will not. It is essential that we take refuge with an understanding of importance of having the best kind of intentions, because obtaining refuge—as well as following the path to the accomplishment of enlightenment—is based on these intentions.

In the second way of taking refuge, we have a sense of the unsatisfactory nature of samsara. We understand that samsara is a choiceless state and that everything in the relative world, including our physical bodies, our friends, and our possessions, is subject to impermanence. Although we would like to see everything as permanent, including the youthfulness of our physical bodies, impermanence creeps up on us gradually. As much as we try to avoid it, we cannot totally separate ourselves from this. Similarly, as much as we would like to be friends with those who are close to us, sometimes friendships end. Everything in worldly life is impermanent. Seeing this impermanence, we see that what impermanence leaves us with is more suffering. We feel suffering when we see the deterioration of our bodies, things around us, and things everywhere in the universe.

Knowing the nature of samsara and with a sense of the possibility of the state of nirvana, the second form of taking refuge is to do so with the intention of liberating ourselves from impermanence and suffering. The objects of refuge are again the same: the Buddha, Dharma, and Sangha. Compared to the first way of taking refuge, this goal is vastly superior because at least there is the knowledge of working toward enlightenment. Still, it is not the best goal, because it is quite selfish. The practitioner has seen suffering and experiences impermanence, and therefore wants liberation for his or her self alone. This is known as the lesser vehicle, or hinayana tradition of taking refuge which we have mentioned earlier. It is called the lesser vehicle because the intention to reach liberation is only for the individual taking refuge. Taking refuge in this way has to do with the influence of the attitudes of those we associate with on the path. Our friends–those with whom we associate–are very important, since they have a great deal of influence on our motivation.

The third attitude in receiving refuge is considered the proper way of receiving refuge in accordance with the particular tradition we are following, namely that of the mahayana ("maha" means greater). With this attitude, we need to learn to overcome the selfish motive of achieving enlightenment for ourselves alone and become quite courageous.

If we associate with the mahayana sangha and are surrounded by the mahayana outlook, we may develop this courage. Those with the mahayana outlook are more courageous because they do not strive toward enlightenment for themselves alone, but toward the enlightenment of all beings.

Compassion and Wisdom

The qualities that make us a proper recipient and practitioner of the mahayana teachings are, first, self-confidence and courage and second, wisdom. The qualities of courage and self-confidence are based on understanding that every living being is experiencing suffering. Whatever suffering we have gone through in the past, tolerable or intolerable, and whatever suffering we are going through now, all living beings suffer in the same way. They may not be experiencing exactly the same kind of pain, but they are always experiencing suffering and unfavorable conditions. All beings, including ourselves, try to avoid such pain and its causes but, since we are lacking in wisdom and are subject to confusion, we still always end up experiencing suffering. This is proof that whatever approach we (as well as others) have used in the past is not the ultimate or proper method.

Knowing that, we should include all living beings in our aspiration toward liberation, not just ourselves. Contemplate the fact that all these living beings, through their confusion, believe that they are on the proper path to happiness but, as a result of the confusion, they are not. By really understanding that everyone has suffering and confusion and is trying to overcome those problems, but that all the methods they have used have not brought them liberation, we will develop the experience of limitless compassion. From this compassion comes the possibility of having the courage and self-confidence to guide all beings—not one or two, but all—to enlightenment. We should work to develop this compassion—and the courage and self-confidence to back it up.

Having developed strong compassion, next is the cultivation of wisdom. Wisdom involves the awareness that providing beings with temporary happiness is not really the solution to their problem. Although it is very important to provide whatever happiness we can for beings, including ourselves, merely working for temporary benefit is not really a solution. Therefore we must develop aspiration for the supreme enlightenment of all beings, which is the union of compassion and wisdom. This union of compassion and wisdom makes us mahayana practitioners.

The union of compassion and wisdom enables us to experience the burning away of our own confusion and obscuration much faster. In the absence of such confusion, the development of realization takes place. The reason that the union of compassion and wisdom leads more rapidly to enlightenment is traditionally compared to the way a bird needs two wings to fly. Similarly, the union of compassion and wisdom enables us to "fly" toward enlightenment. Since we have motivated ourselves to reach enlightenment to benefit and liberate beings, we continue to bring about this benefit in accordance with our goal, and our capacity to benefit beings unfolds immeasurably.

The possibility of working in the proper way toward enlightenment—motivating ourselves in accordance with the mahayana view—is taught to us by our mahayana spiritual friends. As I said, the influence of those we associate with is very significant, and the influence of spiritual friends is quite important in developing the outlook of compassion. There are also those who, without having to be taught, are naturally filled with compassion toward all living beings. That is evidence that this particular individual has practiced in the previous life. His or her obscurations or delusion of mind are less thick. It does not mean there are no obscurations, but there are fewer. As a result of this, these people experience natural compassion toward all beings without being taught. Therefore, we should genuinely rejoice if we have natural compassion toward all living beings.

Each of the countless enlightened beings of the past has achieved enlightenment through this union of compassion and wisdom. Each of the countless enlightened beings of the present achieved that level through the union of compassion and wisdom. And all future enlightened beings will do so in the same way. Thus the integration of these qualities is very important in our lives for the auspicious possibility of future enlightenment. Compassion and wisdom are also referred to as "skillful means" and "primordial wisdom" in Buddhist terminology.

It is the nature of every living being, whether big or small, important or unimportant, to strive for happiness. We yearn not only for a temporary happiness but also for a permanent wellbeing of body and mind. That is not just the goal of human beings; it is very much the goal of every sentient being. We must understand the fact that we all aim toward this one particular purpose.

As I have explained, although the aim of beings is to have happiness, because of their confusion, they do not know how to obtain that happiness and how to avoid the cause of suffering. With that blindness of confusion, although every one of us (including humans, animals, and all other kinds of beings) has the aim of happiness, we end up with suffering.

In the hope of that happiness, we are so preoccupied for our personal wellbeing that we fail to see the needs of other sentient beings. As a result of this preoccupation, no matter how hard we work to provide happiness for ourselves, we always encounter suffering. We are so confused that we really do not know the proper ways of obtaining happiness, and it seems that whatever we do to obtain happiness actually leads us further into the depths of suffering and frustration. The question is this: what led us into such a confused state of mind?

There are two explanations for why we experience this confusion that leads us into suffering. The first is that the habitual patterns of confusion we have built up in previous lives continue in this life, because habitual patterns are very strong. These patterns we have built are very difficult to overcome unless we go through a particular training. Not having overcome them, we experience the continuation of the confusion of habitual patterns, which leads us further into the depths of confusion. Based on the confusion in our past lives, we have engaged in all sorts of harmful activities that lead to the accumulation of negative karma. As a result of that negative karmic accumulation, we experience unfortunate states of being. There are many such inferior births, but the one with which we are most familiar (although there are some that are even more inferior) is the animal realm. An animal's knowledge and human knowledge are very different. An animal's capacity to learn is very limited. I am not saying that animals cannot learn, but their capacity to learn is very limited in comparison to that of human beings. That is one example of the karmic outcome of confusion.

The second reason we experience so much confusion and fail to see the truth is that our associates, the influences around us, are also confused beings. When we are interacting with all these confused beings, along with having our own confused patterns from past lives, these factors in combination strongly influence us to engage in confusion rather than to come out of confusion.

An example of the power of association is this: We all know that the United States is a very civilized country and well-developed in technology. People here are well educated in technical matters. But no one is born fully informed about technology, so why are Americans so well informed about this? It is because your culture is steeped in technology. Since your environment is filled with technology, it is quite familiar to you, and compared with some other cultures you learn about it without much effort. Similarly, the entire world knows that America is advanced in certain ways, but it is very rare to hear of enlightened beings coming from this country. Why have we not heard of American enlightened beings? It is not that you do not have the potential for enlightenment, but rather that you have not had the social environment of enlightened beings whereby you might learn and become familiar with the path. Because of the lack of such enlightened society, so to speak, America is not yet well known for enlightenment.

Despite that fact, you might ask why so many people here are currently interested in the path to enlightenment. It is very obvious that all of you, and all those who are interested in such a path, were connected to that path in a previous life. As a result of that connection in a previous life, there is still a warmth, an interest, drawing you toward this particular subject in this lifetime. Therefore, although the subject of Buddhism has not historically been widespread in the United States, you are intrigued with it and are interested in taking the refuge vow. I feel quite certain that you are completing a journey that you have connected with in a past life. It is very fortunate to be able to connect with whatever you began in a previous life, in order to continue it in this life and hopefully to fulfill it.

The actual process of refuge is based on your state of mind—your mental attitude. When you are receiving the refuge vow, a feeling of joy and acceptance must be present in your mind. If you lack that feeling of joy and acceptance of the refuge, then the vow cannot be fully obtained, because there is blockage or rejection. Taking refuge should bring real joy, because the opportunity to receive the refuge vow—the pure transmission from an unbroken lineage of this vow—is very rare. When you find something that is very rare and precious, naturally you are happy and joyous. You are not only happy and joyous, but also very open and appreciative. That feeling and attitude is essential while taking the refuge vow.

The Three Types of Trust

The proper attitude in taking refuge can be explained in three parts. I am giving these classifications based on my sense that many of you who are reading this are not completely new to the Dharma, and you are not yet enlightened beings either. Because you are in-between, so to speak, you are well prepared to understand these three points.

The first point is acceptance, which means having trust. This trust also has three classifications. The first is clear, open trust. Clear, open trust is based on the knowledge that the possibility of receiving the refuge vow in an unbroken transmission is very rare. Because it is an unbroken transmission, it is also very precious. Therefore you have gratitude toward the master who is providing this refuge and feel very fortunate. That feeling of being fortunate is the open or clear trust.

The second aspect of trust is the trust of aspiration, or longing trust. Longing trust is based on knowing that not only do you want to obtain the refuge, but also that your goal is to practice. You want to accomplish and perfect the path. Your aim in obtaining the refuge is the longing or desire to perfect yourself. You have a desire to eliminate all your confusion, mistakes, and obscurations and develop the qualities of wisdom and enlightenment. This is longing trust.

Third, there is believing trust. Believing trust is defined in this way: you want to accomplish enlightenment, eliminating the obscuration or confusion of the mind, but to do so, you have to have trust in the tradition. Trusting the tradition comes from learning and understanding that each of the countless enlightened beings in the past in India and in Tibet have practiced this particular path. Practicing in this way, they reached what is known as the mahasiddha level, the accomplishment of enlightenment. Seeing that, you have a trust in the path, a trust in the practice itself. It has not only been given to you—it has been widely practiced. Therefore, the last type of trust is believing in the path, the practice itself. Developing these three kinds of trust is essential.

The second main point about proper attitude is understanding that enlightenment belongs to no particular culture, type of individual, or gender. Therefore, it is a mistaken view to think that enlightenment is only possible for, say, Asian people. It is also completely mistaken to think that enlightenment is only possible for men. As long as an individual has the capacity to understand, that individual, whether from the West or East, male or female, has the capacity for enlightenment. Every individual, regardless of which culture they belong to, has different levels or strengths of confusion and obscuration depending upon their individual personality. Some of us may have a particular negative psychological pattern that is very strong; while for others that pattern will be weaker. Similarly, based on individual effort, some people can achieve enlightenment faster with proper effort, and some of us may not progress so quickly, because we are not putting a strong effort into the path.

Whatever qualities we start with, and however motivated and diligent we are, the goal of those on the path is to attain enlightenment. To actually accomplish this, the first thing we need to do is to lay the proper foundation. Taking refuge is indeed the step that lays the foundation.

Then to further cultivate the path of enlightenment, we need to meet all the proper conditions, such as having the qualified spiritual master who can guide us in the proper way of practicing. As we have seen, there are many sidetracks and confused approaches we could take in the spiritual journey. Because of this, and because it takes an accomplished being to guide us properly, the help of a spiritual master who is fully trained in the path of enlightenment is necessary for our progress. Meeting such a person is essential to further cultivate the aspiration of walking the path and reaching its goal.

We sometimes use the term enlightenment in a fairly casual or superficial way in English. It is used to simply mean understanding something you have not understood before. We might say, "I was enlightened by this or that explanation or information." However, enlightenment in the Buddhist tradition has a very precise and profound meaning. It can be explained by looking at the Tibetan term sangye, which means both buddhahood and buddha. The two syllables of sangye each have a meaning. Sang means elimination or purification. What is being eliminated or purified is every sort of negative psychological pattern, confusion, and ignorance. The second syllable, gye, means "blossomed" or "fully developed." In the absence of all confusion and mental obscuration, what develops are the mind's potentials and qualities—qualities such as wisdom and knowledge.

Are these enlightened qualities temporary? No, they are permanent. Once you have eliminated all obscuration and fully experienced or realized your own mind's qualities, you are a fully enlightened being. That is what is meant by sangye. It does not just mean the historical Buddha of our time (Shakyamuni). Sangye means the elimination of faults, confusion, and the full development of wisdom qualities. That is what buddhahood is.

The Refuge Ceremony

This teaching has been intended to give some background as to what taking refuge actually means in terms of the objects of refuge, developing the best kind of motivation and attitude, and the importance of a pure lineage. Some additional information, such as how you should relate to the Buddha, Dharma, and Sangha in daily life, will be presented when you formally participate in the refuge ceremony.

The refuge vow lays the foundation for our spiritual growth as we progress toward enlightenment. That foundation is made possible through the proper mental state or attitude coinciding with the transmission. In keeping with that, a gesture of devotion toward that possibility is an important factor in taking refuge. For that reason, people traditionally make offerings at the time of the refuge ceremony such as butter lamps, incense, or a flower as a gesture of devotion and joy in receiving the vow. It is good to make such offerings, because it brings about the accumulation of merit and is an expression of devotion, which is necessary in receiving refuge. However, if you do not want to do this, there is really no obligation to do so.

Additional instructions or reminders concerning taking refuge are given before the ceremony itself, since having the proper mental attitude during the ceremony is essential for obtaining the refuge transmission. At the time of the ceremony, there is really not much to do. You simply sit, repeat the words of the Tibetan prayers, and you receive the refuge. If you do not know what you are doing, why you are doing it, and what state of mind you should have, then you are simply sitting and repeating an unknown language. Since it is important not only to repeat the words but also to know what you are repeating and what state of mind you should have, I have given this instruction.

If someone participates in the refuge ceremony without any knowledge of refuge, and without even knowing the words they are repeating, we could again use the analogy of the bucket with holes in it. No matter what you put in, it runs out through the holes. If a person has some knowledge of refuge, but is not aspiring toward enlightenment, and if they take refuge with a goal of happiness and prosperity of this and the next life, then they will have refuge, but they will be unable to reach enlightenment, simply because they have not aspired to enlightenment.

To enable you to be a perfect recipient of the refuge vow, I have given a complete explanation of the objects of refuge, and what state of mind you need to have. Particularly, it is important to take the attitude of including all living beings with a sense of compassion and wanting to guide them to liberation. This makes you a very proper vessel, one without any "holes" at all. When you are a proper vessel, even if what you are putting in is a small amount, adding it to the container drop by drop every day, it is possible eventually to fill it up. You are not lacking in a noble goal. In order to become a proper vessel to move toward enlightenment, the foundation of refuge is essential.

Finally, I would like to mention some commitments that go along with taking refuge. The theme that runs through all these commitments is that of maintaining respect for the Three Jewels, but they also involve establishing proper Buddhist attitudes toward beings in general and all religions.

Having taken refuge in the Buddha, you should treat everything that represents the Buddha, such as a statue, with respect. Right down to the smallest statue, image, or picture of enlightened beings, regard them as genuine representations of the Buddha.

Having taken refuge in the Dharma, try not to harm sentient beings intentionally. Instead, help beings as much as you are able. As well, everything that represents the Dharma, such as Buddhist books in any language, should be treated with respect.

Having taken refuge in the Sangha, try to maintain a positive connection with it. Another important point is that we should not take on a sectarian attitude about our affiliation with Buddhism. Those who have taken refuge should not get into disputes as to which religion, lineage, or community is better or worse. Instead, you should respect every religion. The Buddhist attitude is one of respect for all communities of religious practitioners, not just our own.

Whatever your immediate or future participation in this tradition may be, I aspire that it be of genuine benefit to you. Developing the intention to take refuge is a very virtuous action, so I would like to thank each of you from the bottom of my heart for the interest you have taken in this subject.

Questions and Answers

Buddhist teachings often include question and answer sessions, because simply receiving information is not enough. We need to interact with the teacher, and it is important to clear up any doubts and uncertainties you may we have. This is particularly true in the case of the very auspicious personal step of taking refuge. Once your questions are answered, there will be a sense of ease in taking refuge. As long as there is uncertainty and doubt, that could interfere with having a proper state of mind or attitude during the ceremony. These questions are examples of those asked during the teachings on refuge that make up this book.

Question: I am interested in the relationship between self-confidence and compassion. In our culture, and, I guess, in all cultures, we often see people who become overly self-confident. A lot of people who we think of as being self-confident become arrogant and seem to lack the qualities of compassion. Sometimes compassion is associated with someone who is rather passive and meek, so I am interested to know more about this relationship.

Rinpoche: There is the possibility of confusing self-confidence and arrogance, so I must make it clear that the two qualities are very different.

The kind of self-confidence that is needed in the mahayana outlook is the confidence, first of all, that you want to provide happiness to not only a few people, but all sentient beings; and second, that you are also able to do so. Seeing that possibility in yourself is self-confidence. With arrogance, you feel good about yourself, but you look down on others. With self-confidence, you do not look down on anyone; you believe you have the capacity to help everyone and that everyone is equal. In that sense, the feelings are very different.

Concerning compassion, according to the dharmic understanding, it is explained as realizing that the greatest deception is self-centeredness. Therefore, we try to break through that self-centeredness, realizing that we are not the only ones who are experiencing suffering, but that every living being experiences suffering. We are not the only ones trying to obtain happiness—every living being is longing for that. With that knowledge, we try to do whatever possible within our physical capacity to benefit others, and spiritually we try to grow and develop our capacities. The union of spiritual and physical benefit for others is accomplished through having such a true knowledge of compassion.

Question: Having done some Dharma practice, I have felt inspired to formally take the refuge vow, especially in terms of refuge in the Sangha. However, right at this moment I am feeling a lot of emotional turmoil. I guess I am doubting whether I will make a proper recipient for the vows.

Rinpoche: If it were the case that we became completely purified of negative qualities the moment we receive Dharma instruction or begin to do practice, then further practice would not be necessary. That is not very likely. Since we are not totally pure, teachings and instruction are presented as an ongoing inspiration. As long as some inspiration has arisen in your mind, along with some sense of respect for the Sangha and other objects of refuge, these basic qualities of your attitude make you a suitable vessel to take refuge.

Question: You spoke about the importance of the union of wisdom and skillful means. I was wondering if you could explain a little bit on how a person actually puts that unity into practice.

Rinpoche: I will explain the idea of the union of skillful means and wisdom in a very simple way here. Skillful means is doing whatever practice you do, or virtuous activity you engage in, with an altruistic mind. This means your intention is that you are engaging in that positive action for the benefit of all sentient beings. Then the question is, what sort of benefit are we intending? If we intend for them to have the ultimate realization of buddhahood—rather than the benefit of temporary worldly relief—that is wisdom.

Of course, this topic can be explained from many different angles, but to present it simply, the altruistic mind of including all sentient beings is skillful means and aspiring for their spiritual enlightenment is wisdom.

Question: Could you elaborate on how compassion and wisdom work together?

Rinpoche: The union of compassion and wisdom is like the union of skillful means and wisdom. Skillful means is actually equivalent to compassion. For example, if when you take the refuge vow, if you have the attitude, "I am taking the refuge vow for the benefit of all living beings," that is compassion. In order to include all living beings in your heart, you must have some compassion, understanding, and acceptance. That acceptance and understanding becomes a part of compassion, which is skillful means.

If you do not understand the ultimate goal or ultimate destination is enlightenment, and if you think, "I want to take refuge for the benefit of all living beings," but enlightenment is not included there, then you are missing the wisdom part because you are thinking in terms of temporary benefit. You can be helpful to beings, but whatever help you provide is subject to deterioration, and the beings can return again to further suffering. To accomplish their being truly finished with suffering, we aspire to establish all of them in the ultimate realization of buddhahood.

Compassion does not mean that we include only people we know personally, or those of our own nationality. It does not mean that we are only thinking of liberating human beings. It means including every living being—birds, insects, and every other sort of being. That is unconditional compassion.

Question: What should we do to inwardly prepare for the actual ceremony of taking refuge? Is taking refuge an act of just receiving, or is there an offering at the same time? At the time of taking refuge, where should our focus be concerning our defilements? Finally, at the time of taking refuge, is there a particular center (chakra) that we are receiving it through and should keep open?

Rinpoche: Getting an explanation and understanding of refuge is a very important part of the preparation, so we are doing that now. Mainly the preparation for the refuge involves the knowledge of what refuge is, along with developing the proper attitude, the proper state of mind. That is why I have stressed developing the proper mental state, which involves the attitude that we are not just taking refuge for our own liberation or enlightenment, but rather we take refuge in the Buddha, the Dharma, and the Sangha for the enlightenment of all sentient beings. If you have that in mind, that is very much a sufficient preparation. In addition to that, there is the actual repetition of prayers, led by the refuge master during the refuge ceremony, and some prostrations to do, which the refuge master will tell you to do at the proper time.

Refuge really means that we are simply committing ourselves to engage in positive activities. The main point of it is the commitment. We are committing to positive activities because our goal is to liberate all beings, not only from temporary pain or suffering, but to the ultimate realization of buddhahood, which is permanent. With that attitude we are committing to engage in the proper activities (physically, verbally, and mentally) that benefit all living beings.

The root of all mental afflictions is ignorance, so the whole goal in taking refuge is to eliminate ignorance and give birth to awareness. We aim to eliminate ignorance because it is the root. By focusing on the root, we do not have to aim toward the many branches. By having pure awareness, we can be of tremendous benefit to ourselves as well as to others. For example, right now many people are not very aware of the intense psychological suffering of beings. We are all aware of the physical suffering, but beings go through psychological suffering that we are not aware of. We are unaware of that because of ignorance.

Another aspect of ignorance is that, although all sentient

beings have the enlightened essence, we fail to realize it. Therefore, the goal of establishing all beings in enlightenment involves removing everyone's root mental affliction, ignorance. In the absence of that ignorance we are all enlightened, because we all have the enlightened essence.

In this refuge ceremony, which is the very beginning of the path of Buddhism, there are really no chakras or centers to concentrate on. Simply having openness of mind and the altruistic attitude is sufficient. Later on, in the advanced stages of practice, based on each individual's readiness, there are centers or chakras that are visualized or concentrated on, but not here.

Question: Can you address what it means to take vows and develop an affiliation to this particular lineage as compared to the others? How do you feel about continuing practices from other traditions simultaneously in addition to this, if there is no underlying fundamental conflict?

Rinpoche: The definition of the vow in this tradition is that, from the moment you receive the vow, you are committing yourself, thinking, "From today onward, I will exert myself to benefiting and establishing all beings in enlightenment." That is the commitment. Since you have said, for example, "I will exert myself for benefiting and liberating all living beings," then your responsibility in accordance with the vow is doing anything that is beneficial, doing anything that is harmless.

Therefore, I cannot speak specifically about different traditions, but if any tradition that you are practicing is aimed to benefit living beings, it is perfectly fine to continue it. However, there are many religions that believe in sacrificing life and so forth. If you are practicing such things, then you are totally going against this vow, so that is not advisable. Other than that, any tradition that seems to be benefiting, aspiring to help others, you are free to continue.

Question: Within the different lineages of Tibetan tradition, is it just the fact that they have been handed down through different people that differentiates them, or are there fundamental differences in them and how they developed? What are the differences between them?

Rinpoche: In the various branches of Tibetan Buddhism, concerning the idea of the union of compassion and wisdom, there is no difference at all. Concerning the objects of refuge—the Buddha, Dharma and Sangha—there is no difference at all. The teaching, or the transmission, originated from the same source, the Buddha, and the goal is the same: enlightenment.

What is different between the different traditions in some cases is the presentation of the order of the practice. It has been set up slightly differently, according to the insights of the various skilled teachers, so there are what are called different traditions. It is like a father having four sons. If you ask any of them who their father is, the answer will be the same, but they might live differently, and they might have different numbers of children. It is similar to that.

Question: Could you explain the difference between the refuge vow and the bodhisattva vow? What I am hearing about the proper mahayana attitude in taking refuge reminds me of what I have heard about the bodhisattva vow.

Rinpoche: There is quite a big difference. The difference is based on the seriousness of your responsibility. In taking refuge, the goal is that you want to liberate yourself and all sentient beings, as I have said. Right now, however, you do not have that capacity, so you are asking the assistance of the sources of refuge, those who do have the capacity—the Buddha, the Dharma and the Sangha—to fulfill your goal.

To put it another way, you want the Buddha, Dharma, and Sangha to include you among them, so to speak. This still involves the notion of wanting to benefit living beings, but you are seeking someone else's help to do that. The bodhisattva vow is that you are taking the responsibility alone: "I will liberate all sentient beings." Taking on that complete personal responsibility is what makes the bodhisattva vow different.

As a second analogy for the refuge and the bodhisattva vow, I could use myself as an example. Since I am a Tibetan, taking refuge would be similar to my applying to become a citizen of the United States. Once I become a citizen of the United States, I am an American; I have the rights of an American. Therefore, I have not only the rights of an American, but also the responsibility to follow the laws of America. The bodhisattva vow is a bit like seeking to become President of the United States. It is in the same country, but the responsibility is much, much greater.

Question: I am a vegetarian, and I do not see how eating meat fits in with the principle of not harming. It seems to be a conflict with that, which confuses and bothers me.

Rinpoche: In order to answer that particular question, we have to be quite logical. We cannot be biased. We have to be open to all situations. First of all, I have a tremendous respect for vegetarians. In Tibet, where I was brought up, vegetarianism was not possible. Since I grew up eating meat, I do not do well on a vegetarian diet—I feel very bad without meat in my diet.

Therefore, it is not that I am unaware of it. Each time I have to take a meal, it is impossible to overlook. Eating meat is indeed evidence that you have harmed a being. There is that particular flesh you are eating, so it is very obvious.

At the same time, we have to understand that we are in samsara. Whatever we do in samsara—even if we are working toward enlightenment—we cannot achieve realization right at the moment we begin aspiring in that direction. It takes quite a long time from the moment we get intrigued with the idea of enlightenment to the achievement of it. As we traverse the path, we have to survive. There are many different ways to survive in samsara, but I do not think that there is any way of surviving in samsara that is really wholesome. For example, when you boil a pot of water; you are killing beings in there. According to Buddhism, the physical size does not matter. Beings are beings, whether small or big. You are killing thousands of beings by boiling the pot of water.

Then let's take the example of a vegetarian. It is not obvious you are harming beings when you are eating vegetables, because no flesh is being eaten. But when the farmer plows or cultivates the ground, they are killing many insects. Insects are living beings. The fact is that all forms of farming kill countless beings to produce our food. Even as vegetarian, you are unable to live without harming others.

It is not a matter of being vegetarian or nonvegetarian. It is the nature of samsara. This particular case is an example of why, as Buddhists, we speak of the nature of samsara being suffering. Although we all have the intention not to harm any being, for our survival we have to eat and drink, and in anything we do there are living beings' lives involved.

Question: About the confusion, neurosis, and suffering you spoke about that we all live with, and the fact that it is intensified because it has been going on for so many lifetimes and because we live in an environment where others are in the same situation. I was wondering if you could say more about the original cause—how it got started and why it caught on the way it seems to have.

Rinpoche: Both samsara and confusion are considered to be beginningless in Buddhism, so there is no real how or why as to the beginning of samsara or how we became caught in confusion. That is a big part of confusion, because not being able to see that fact is in itself confusion. The positive side of confusion is that there can be an end to it. If you practice, and if you get some realization, and if you achieve enlightenment, that is the end of confusion. We cannot really talk about a beginning though.

Many traditions teach that whatever we experience in this lifetime, whether good or bad, happiness or sadness, is the outcome of good or bad activity in past lives, and whatever good or bad you do in this life affects the next life, and so forth. It is possible we may have been great practitioners in the past and, therefore, our neurosis or confusion may not be so strong in this life, and our ability to understand and achieve enlightenment will be greater than it is for others. This is because of our previous connections.

Other than that, the nature of confusion is that it has no particular beginning. Various religions in the world, thinking that they do need to talk about a beginning to confusion, tend to blame it on a superior being, saying they have punished us, and therefore we are in this particular situation. But Buddhism does not teach that there is anybody punishing us except our own karma, which is confusion.

Question: Could you discuss how we can eliminate some of our confusion, in particular concerning our associations with others?

Rinpoche: The beginning of the elimination of confusion starts from the moment we take refuge. Why were we not able to eliminate confusion in the past, prior to having knowledge of the sources of refuge? It was because of the preoccupation with self, the selfish attitudes and self-centeredness, that prevented us from eliminating our own confusion. Thus we were not really able to work for the elimination of others' confusion either.

The process of the elimination of confusion starts with an impartial state of mind. In the past, even if we have had a feeling for others, it was very limited and personal in scope. We might have had some compassion, perhaps wanting to provide happiness to our family, but probably not to all people. As long as it is "my family," it is very selfish. As long as it is, "my friends," "I want my friends to have good health and happiness," we become very possessive of "my" rather than "them." We have not included all beings in our compassion. The attitude is in a sense altruistic, but it is a very selfish altruism. There are some people who go beyond the boundaries of family, relatives, and friends, saying "my country," "my people," but still it is limited to that, rather than for all beings. There is no impartial state of thinking.

We are able to eliminate confusion the moment we have an impartial feeling of liberating all beings, without bias toward "my family, my friends, my countrymen," or anything. It is a matter of not only having compassion toward human beings, but also having it for all living beings. We start to eliminate confusion the moment we understand this. At present, people may think enlightenment is somewhere way up in the sky. When we talk about achieving enlightenment, they think they are going to another planet! We are not going anywhere at all; we are right where we are. Enlightenment simply means the elimination of our neurotic patterns of mind, the mental afflictions.

The second thing about confusion is that previously we did not work toward achieving perfection of the mind. Typically, we have been caught up in focusing on external concerns—our physical body, our immediate circumstances, and our ambitions. I am not saying you should not have physical wellbeing and personal success, but training the mind is very important. We have not worked to eliminate the errors and mistakes of the mind, which is why we are not enlightened. Therefore, we need to understand that enlightenment means eliminating mental mistakes or errors. Enlightenment is not another realm. It is the absence of all delusion and confusion. The altruistic mind of benefiting all living beings is completely impartial, and that is the way to eliminate confusion.

Question: Sometimes we have compassion for people, but whatever we do winds up being harmful for them in some way. It is not in their best interest. Without being enlightened, how can we have the wisdom to know whether we are really acting in their interest, or if it is more our own interest that is motivating us?

Rinpoche: Real compassion is such that it is always harmless. Even if there is some mixture of self-interest in the compassion, still it is harmless. As a beginner in the practice, since one's mind is not fully pure right now, self-interest may be mixed in. If you really want to know if your compassion is authentic compassion, if the being for whom you have compassion reacts badly and even does something negative to you in response, and even then you have no anger—then you have authentic compassion. Compassion itself is the remedy for anger.

Question: Can you share with us what goes on while you are choosing a refuge name? Does the name have a meaning?

Rinpoche: I normally choose a name with the intention that you will understand the meaning of that name, and my aspiration or prayer is that you will fulfill that meaning. Each of you will have a different name and thus a different meaning.

Question: There are a lot of differences between Western culture and traditional Buddhist culture. Is it necessary to believe in or understand all of the cultural beliefs that seem to go along with Buddhism in order to be a good practitioner?

Rinpoche: First of all, the essence of Dharma is not cultural at all. And culture is really not the key to enlightenment. There are many academic teachers who have mastered Eastern culture and have not even reached the beginning of enlightenment. Cultural beliefs do not bring people to the enlightened state. No matter what culture we belong to, everyone wants to enjoy happiness and get rid of the cause of suffering. It is not a matter of East or West. Knowing that, if you practice with the intention to provide well-being, goodness, enlightenment, and freedom from suffering and the cause of suffering impartially for every being, then you can be a good practitioner, even if you have no knowledge of Eastern culture at all.

Question: Could you elaborate on the importance of spiritual friends and how a person can develop and maintain a relationship with a spiritual friend in contemporary society?

Rinpoche: A beginner on the spiritual path is somewhat like an infant. The upbringing of the infant is based on what sort of environment and family he or she is brought up with. We are very easily influenced, just as an infant is, and we are very dependent on those who are spiritually well balanced, those who we call spiritual friends. With their example of devotion to the spiritual path, we learn as we grow in that path.

For example, if you are living with a group of people who smoke, you are very likely to be influenced by the smokers and start smoking. The same could be true if you associate with heavy drinkers or drug users. We are influenced by those around us, based on the strength of the influence in our environment.

Spiritual growth is very similar. Right now, being like infants, we have to depend on the spiritual friend. Although the Dharma is very new in the United States, there are quite a few people who are devoted to spiritual practice. It is helpful to be around such people so we can lead and inspire each other in virtuous activities, becoming very strong-minded in the goal. Once you have become strong and balanced in the spiritual path yourself then even if you associate with nonvirtuous people, they cannot influence you.

Until you become that strong, a spiritual friend is necessary. If you are around practitioners (preferably with masters, but they are not always available) even ordinary practitioners can help inspire each other not to engage in harmful activities of body, speech, and mind. Together, many practitioners may be able to make a perfect environment for the practice. It is like having a single log of wood. It is very difficult to make a fire with just one piece of wood, but with a collection of many logs together, you can have a big fire. Likewise, even if you are not all realized, even a collection of beginners in the Dharma can develop a good practice together. That would be a positive thing to look for.

The Refuge Prayer

༄༅། །སངས་རྒྱས་ཆོས་དང་ཚོགས་ཀྱི་མཆོག་རྣམས་ལ། །
SANG GYE CHÖ DANG TSHOK KYI CHOK NAM LA
In the Buddha, Dharma, and Sangha,

བྱང་ཆུབ་བར་དུ་བདག་ནི་སྐྱབས་སུ་མཆི། །
JANG CHUP BAR DU DAK NI KYAP SU CHI
I take refuge until I reach enlightenment.

བདག་གིས་སྦྱིན་སོགས་བགྱིས་པའི་བསོད་ནམས་ཀྱིས། །
DAK GI JIN SOK GYI PAY SÖ NAM KYI
By the merit of practicing generosity and the other perfections,

འགྲོ་ལ་ཕན་ཕྱིར་སངས་རྒྱས་འགྲུབ་པར་ཤོག །
DRO LA PHEN CHIR SANG GYE DRUP PAR SHOK
May I attain full awakening for the benefit of all beings.

Karma Triyana Dharmachakra

Karma Triyana Dharmachakra (KTD) monastery in Woodstock, New York, the North American Seat of His Holiness Karmapa, offers an annual weekend teaching on refuge which concludes with a refuge ceremony. The refuge ceremony is also normally conducted at KTD and affiliated centers any time an empowerment is scheduled. Please contact the center in advance. Visit the web site of Karma Triyana Dharmachakra for information about Khenpo Karthar Rinpoche's teaching schedule and affiliated centers worldwide at www.kagyu.org.

Whatever merit has been accumulated through the publication of this edition is dedicated to the benefit of all beings, and especially to the long life of Khenpo Karthar Rinpoche and the flourishing of the authentic Dharma throughout the world.

Acknowledgments

The original version of this text was produced at Heart Center KTC under the direction of Michael & Margaret Erlewine and is based on two teachings:
"The Meaning of Refuge," given at Chicago KTC in January 1981
Translated by Ngödup Tsering Burkhar; Transcribed by Robert Martinez, Edited by Robert Martinez and David McCarthy and
"A Teaching on Refuge," given at KTD Monastery in April 1990
Translated by Chöjor Radha; Transcribed by Malinda McCain
Edited by Linda Clark and David McCarthy
Edited by David McCarthy

First Edition, 2002

Cover & Book Design by Louise Light
Cover Image of Shakyamuni Buddha Courtesy of Namse Bangdzo Bookstore
Cover & Chapter Line Art Courtesy of Michael Erlewine
Back Cover Photo of Khenpo Karthar Rinpoche Courtesy of KTD
Special Thanks to Lois DePiesse, Lama Jacqueline DeBray,
Peter Van Deurzen, Michael & Margaret Erlewine, Ilfra Halley, David Kendall and Beatrice Lin Kendall, Chojor Radha, and all those who contributed to the original version.

Second Edition, 2013

Maureen McNicholas and Peter van Deurzen, KTD Publications

May All Beings Be Happy